A Brief Infinity

Poems

Marlaina Donato

Ekstasis Multimedia
Blairstown, New Jersey

A BRIEF INFINITY Copyright ©2012 Marlaina Donato All Rights Reserved. Printed in the United States of America. No part of this book may be used or reproduced in any way without written permission from the publisher except in the case of brief quotations embodied in articles and reviews.

Ekstasis Multimedia: www.booksandbrush.net

ISBN-13:978-0615717906
ISBN-10:061571790X

Photography and design: Marlaina Donato

For my mother, Winifred, Madonna of my Heart-
for her luminous beauty and wisdom;
Thank you for being the light that never blows out
after all the others have. You are the sun I aspire to.

For my husband, Joe- my beloved and soul-divided…
for every minute of every day of this beautiful life. I love you.

Beauty's Chord

Genesis

Morning white

New snow

Canvas

Paper

Slipping along the stark incline of possibility

Boots hesitate to violate a virgin meadow

The brush pauses before plunging into naked grain

The pen trembles with words

The heart lingers between beats

In a tundra of ember

Fearing the wasteland

Of stillborn could-have-beens

White morning

New Snow

Canvas

Paper

Purity of pain that urges us to begin

More difficult than the middle or The End

"Begin," the New whispers, "Begin."

Autumn

After the fields are combed and the orchards are bare,

Autumn tarries with tears in her eyes.

She stains the forests with her auburn hair

And blows out the fire flies.

Her hands ache from harvest labor, and she longs for sleep.

Adorned in the amber of October fires,

She waits until November to weep

And sings in the cricket choirs.

Only the melancholy glimpse her face

As she weaves misty scarves through the maple's drowsy eaves.

She cools the nights, but warm is her embrace.

Then with one last leap of strength, she takes the leaves.

Ambrosia

Drink from the deep, my Soul,

And taste the silver of its surface.

Thirsty Soul, out of density, destiny,

Fly!

Drink the nectar of the night;

Touch the blue flame of the winds, heaven's pulse.

Dissolve into the dawn, singing crystal.

Shimmering Self, into the universes within,

Fly!

Fly the speed of stillness.

Let your heart be a bow against Beauty's chord.

Drink from the deep, my Soul,

Drink the deep and the silver of its surface.

Fly!

Fly the speed of stillness.

A Year

Morning is dappled with memories

Of that year when we lived

Amid shivering oak trees

In a house with a red door;

The year you taught me how to make a fire,

And I felt more accomplished

Than if I had saved a drowning world;

The year mornings were jarred by the banter of ravens,

And we drank spiced cocoa and plotted the future.

It was the year I cried myself to sleep,

And you prayed that we would live;

The year we huddled against circumstance

And clung to the hope of spring.

As the years descend like early snow,

That year lives within me,

The year we lived amid shivering oak trees

In a house with a red door.

Twenty-Something

She is the serpent's sister

With denim hips reciting the names of many lovers

She moves with the ease of blowing sands

As she shifts against the half-open door

Inhaling admiration from her latest cigarette

Exhaling alibis into the indifferent air

What illusion of wisdom in her beauty

As I sit here knowing better

Knowing bitter

The young envying the young

Resolution

This life

Striving to be an ocean…

Immense

Constant

Unbroken

This life

Striving to be a forest…

Wild

Fruitful

Resourceful

Let this life

Be what it is- a desert, a barren womb

Until unexpected rain

A brief infinity of flowers

Beauty out of nothingness

Then back into nothingness

Never repeated

Magma

A red leaf stains the wind, a drop of summer's blood.

While there is still time,

While there is still singing in the fields,

Listen

To the sonnet bound inside my fist,

The scream your eyes forge in me.

Before the veins of youth shrivel under snow,

Listen

While I sing your thorns back to you,

Sing the gold pain of your breath,

Sing the magma inside the steel.

Listen…

It is yours, this blood song.

Wounds

Refugees of the internal war,

We seek shelter here tonight.

Our souls are shattered flames

While the stars remain indifferent.

Wisdom is a bitter cup,

And we have drunk until sickness.

We love until pain

And ecstasy again

Explodes in the blood.

How our wounds find each other,

Open and too deep for resolution;

Love, too fragile for our rage

Can only live an hour.

Dark Wind

New Boots

Walking down the street, rhythm of heels

Feeling dangerous

And bold as a Chihuahua

Barking at a St. Bernard

From behind a fence

Love's Labor

Across a bed wet with sun, we love in the light.

Our bodies praying fire, we ride the day

Until I rest my ear against your heart

And shadows descend like gray birds across your skin.

We have loved well this day,

Labored well in Beauty's house.

We have loved well this day,

This day in forever.

Ascent

Plucked from the bosom of ideals, he meets death alone

Beneath the stars.

On scorching soil, all is forgotten-

Enemy

Cause

Strategy;

All is eclipsed

In a single thought- that of the blond-haired son

Who has his father's eyes.

An eon of minutes

And then sudden flight

Into infinity;

As blazing and focused as a flare into darkness,

A soul ascends

Through smoke,

Over fire.

Home.

Dew

There is neither smile nor twin face
Upon which to press my cheek to your memory;
No voice among man, bird, or wind
That can harmonize with my remembrance.

Upon which dream have you embarked?
Tell me…so my sleeping heart may wake
To find your eyes again
Somewhere on Death's stormless course
On the night-blackened deep.

Upon which sunbeam to you skip barefoot?
Tell me…so these shackles of sorrow
May unfold wings drunk with light.

Within which flower do you leave a kiss?
Tell me…so I may drink the dew there and quench my life.

A Garden

White iris, the brides of the garden,
Toss veils of shadow against the wall.
Our hands wrist-deep in soil,
Whisper promises of roots and flowers
While the tulips flare their Gypsy skirts,
And the fountain sings in a language
Only the lilies know.
Winters from now,
I will take these out of my bag of memories
And shake off the years
To taste dappled days scented with cedar.
And flowers, well-versed in their mother's origins,
Will tell stories about ladies wrist-deep in soil
Who had faith in seeds.

Liturgy

After a long day's rain,

The night is awash with spirits.

Twilight is a sapphire

Faceted by the hands of Deity.

Tree, grass, wanderer…

And all that have longed reach heavenward.

Stillness is sovereign

In the Liturgy of Hours;

And the soul, splintered and scattered,

Gathers unto itself again.

Nomad

My hands travel your night sands;

You shiver in the dark wind of my longing,

Lover of cinnamon and amber,

Lover of a thousand deserts

My soul has traveled.

Sing your hunger in tones of lapis;

Dance the dawn between my thighs.

Shake the centuries from your hair

And teach me the language of sudden rain

On the thousand deserts

My soul has traveled.

Solstice

Calligraphy of branches

Etched on the morning's snowy paper

Raven landing

Punctuation

Sunset

Her outstretched arms
Are the last rays to pierce the trees.
She gilds the West's windswept wings.
Over her bronze shoulder, her palette swings;
She paints the clouds. She mantles the seas.

She turns down the sun's amber sheet
And tucks in bird and flower.
She silhouettes hill and tower
And dances with sovereign feet.

She braids tangerine ribbon through
Heaven's cerulean hair
And blushes the surf's pristine cheek.
She puts the thrush to sleep
Then flees on her dusky mare.

Angel's Wing

Grace

Peace

Is

Having

The river's wisdom-

To carry the rain on your back with grace

Knowing the sea is your destiny.

Red Mittens

December air, the smoke of a fire
Memory on impatient wings
My father cutting wood
Face flushed like roses
The scent of oak
And the sound
Of the blade scattering splinters
Memory of my hands in red mittens
Grasping logs on the bottom stair
And the gentle voice
Telling me the air promised snow
And not to take more than I could lift
December air, the smoke of a fire
Memory on impatient wings
My father on a winter day

Snow on a Raven's Wing

A soul descends to the university of lies
And dons a robe of desire.
Ignorant of its former wings, crawls through fire,
Without wisdom and without eyes.

The ink runs dry in the writer's pen,
And the unfulfilled, white paper of a life
Lies waiting.
A widowed heart listens for familiar footsteps
That will never return.
Swift hours fall lame;
When will ecstasy again pain the senses?

All unfulfillments, errors, and transgressions,
Death satisfies, rectifies,
And apologizes for.

Hear Death's silent voice
Loudest in Joy's smug laughter…

Oh, hear Her sing.

With celibate hands, She mends all things.

Oh, hear Her sing…

Softly as snow on a raven's wing.

All that is born innocent

Dies soiled by living

Until Death cries and purifies

With cold fire.

Hear Death's silent voice

Loudest in Joy's smug laughter…

Oh, hear Her sing.

With celibate hands

She mends all things.

Oh, hear Her sing…

Softly as snow on a raven's wing.

All words left unsaid, all songs unheard,

All crystal summits reached for in vain

Are Death's courtesies, all of these.

Mists haunt November brooks,

Phantoms of summer past

Grieving the turning of time.

The drowsy bramble displays pearls of rain

On thorned, fruitless fingers.

The last generation of leaves

Is buried along the roadside,

A pauper's grave, crowded and wet.

Fire berries burn in scarlet hope

Until the first dispassionate snow

Fatally stings.

Can you hear Death's silent voice

In Joy's smug laughter?

Oh, hear Her sing;

Can you hear Her sing?

With celibate hands

She mends all things, all things.

Oh, hear Her sing

Softly…as snow on a raven's wing.

Heartwood

Lightning came

No one heard the fall

I am here tangled in the memory of roots

In thick underbrush, moss covering over

Earth reclaiming her own as it should be

Yet in the wet hours of night

I think of you, you of salt and earth

You who would take my heart and carve a new dream

You who would sand the splinters of fire

And buff my hard edges of mistrust

You who would take me and be gentle

With nail and rhythm of hammer

I think of you and your hands

Their sun-burned terra cotta and white stains of paint

Splattered like careless prayers

Sometimes heartwood must rot

And the carpenter's hands must remain empty

Each needing the other, a thousand seasons apart

Scarcely aware of what could be built in another time.

Winter

Embraced by the North's infertile breath,
Winter arrives with yew braided in her hair.
Barren, she is akin to death;
'Tis poison fruit her sable tresses bear.

Look for her eyes in the blue of December twilights,
And listen quietly for her trailing gowns.
When the moon wears a halo of whispered white,
'Tis then she empties her purse of frosted down.

She bejewels the trees when the year is new
And buffs the lake for sharpened silver blades.
Morning sun ignites her prism's hue,
'Tis why we forgive her heart of spades.

Seraph

Summer morning

Sound of the piano drifting outside

Four years old, watching clouds

And listening to my mother's fingers dance over ivory

Voice shimmering like an angel's wing

Four years old, watching clouds

And reaching toward blue

Trying to touch heaven to my mother's voice

Gratitude

Hectic day, counting problems

Traffic jam, looking at the time

Hectic day, counting seconds

Traffic jam, funeral procession

Five minutes of cars with lights turned on

In honor of the dead

Seventeen year old girl laughing just two days ago

Mother burying her oldest

As May blossoms blow away into green

Mother not knowing what to do

With the prom dress

Or the dreams

Traffic jam, pause for silence

Beautiful day, counting blessings

Nostalgia

Only yesterday
Your hair caught the sun in its golden net
And your five-year-old smile was a blushing flower.
Only tonight,
After frolicking in your memory,
I realized you must be a woman now;
In a dream's passing, you were gone,
Golden child haloed by sunbeams.

Somewhere, far from time's insidious hand,
The children we all once were
Play in the wind-scented grass of a loved one's memory.

White Fragrance

Lineage

April holds out her cup of joy;

We drink her nectar of dark and light,

Sweet and deep fermented days

Dizzy with color and loud with desire.

We are in love, and so too, the world.

We languish in lush oasis,

Honeycomb bodies dripping with satiety.

Our lineage is infinite-

Lovers upon lovers flow in our veins.

This is our blooming hour of sustenance,

Our turn in eternity.

Microcosm

With the silken threads of the seasons,

Gaia weaves the tapestry of our days.

At the loom of Time, she braids the ages-

Each leaf, tree, stone…a thread.

Each heartbeat, breath, vision…a thread.

One thread severed from the whole,

Death of Nature, death of man.

Signature

Snow-dusted twilight, white constancy
Neighbor's cinnamon cat
Tip-toeing toward dinner
Pattern of paw prints
Across the porch

Chestnut Ribbon

I remember a woman
Drying her hair in the sun;
In a stream it dried in the wind
And shone like chestnut ribbon
Down her spine.
Fresh from sleep, I'd startle her thoughts,
And she'd give me a slice
Of her morning orange.
I remember a woman
Gliding in a cranberry gown
With lily-of-the-valley sweetening her steps.
I was nine
When I became aware of her beauty.

These sacred memories of my mother return
With the newness of impatient surf
Whenever I glimpse a crimson dress
Or smell oranges in the sun.

Legacy

Only a tree knows the life of a leaf-
The bud's crimson cradle
And the first brushstroke of green
On April's rain-dark canvas.
Only the tree knows the life of a leaf-
The summit of summer
Leading to long-awaited autumn;
Only in a leaf's gold death
Is its purpose fulfilled.
Its idle hours are cast into a breath of wind
And seasons of preparation unfurl into flight.
And the tree, having never had wings,
Births wings
And watches her children fly.

Oleander

My words are flowers in virgin light;

When you see me, you only see white fragrance.

You do not see the dark root,

The root so filled with want

It would poison your hand.

Crush the morning;

Rip me from the ground.

Spill my juices until they burn the flesh

And I can finally touch the bone.

Snow Angels

The snow carves a cold blade
Into an onyx night;
We walk against the wind's diamond breath
Along the road lost hours ago.
I lean inside your corduroy
As we navigate the drifts in zigzag laughter.
"Do you remember our first winter?" you ask,
Folding me closer inside your coat
Until our footsteps tangle.
"Blueberry pancakes in bed, your velvet jacket," I whisper
memories.
We carve a road of laughter and wrestle in the white,
Your body burning over me.
Long pause, deep kiss, and over your shoulder,
Parting clouds
And a single star.

Vessel

There are nights inside of me

Stained with wounding

There are gardens of thorn

And mornings without hope

There are death camps

And ghosts of old hungers

I come to you hollowed, my soul carved by fire

I arrive, a phoenix after inferno

New and naked and trembling

I come carved by night

Empty to hold the dawn to your lips

Empty to hold the wine

That only comes

After the pain of the harvest

Homeland

Down a river

Of rapids and stone

Naked, unarmed, and tossed

Bound to flesh and bone

In search of an earthly title

Far from banks of rest

Enslaved to pride's bitter bridle

With wisdom the rocks scold and tame

Until the spirit directs its sail

Back to the sea from whence it came

Bright Darkness

Prayer

Give me a star,

And my life will bloom a heaven.

Give me a crumb,

And my spirit will find a feast.

Give me a drop,

And my heart will hold an ocean.

Give me a word,

And my tongue will sing the ages.

Give me now,

And my soul will be immortal.

November

Where's your hat, hearty little bird?

You color the winter-quiet like roses in the snow.

Not even wind-drift alters your bobbing flight.

The storm fills earth's November cup

Like blossoms falling in June,

Sparing your nest hidden in the spruce.

Gather your food, snowy little bird;

The voice of winter calls.

When you pass by my window,

I will remember roses.

Departure

I am going into the unknown,

Into the bright darkness within.

It has taken death to open the dream

Between worlds.

Do not look for me.

I am where the heart beats,

Where the blood flows;

I am inside you.

We are so close we are separated

By thousands of miles of consciousness.

Mentor

At this scarlet hour,

Quiet tree laden with blowing embers,

Teach me the song of crimson;

My rooted brother, sing your mantra of fire

And then stand before your lover, Winter.

Show me how to burn

And blind the air with light

Then live to tell my story in green.

Kindred

Cat purring to my heartbeat

Moment of perfect understanding

No explanation why I read poetry

And never read directions

Or wear moccasins in the winter

No explanation of her taste in mice

Or what she dreams of in the sun

Kindred spirits

Eden Unbarred

Willful curve of brow, chiseled grace of hand,
Bare strength of shoulder…
In my thoughts, you are a god tonight.
Each light and shadow of you is sacred ground;
Allow me this hour of idolatry.
I drink the river's thirst, and the river drinks of me.
River Lethe, Lover Lethe,
Naked and trembling upon your shore, I drink
And forget I've drunk before,
Forever wanting more
Of you.
Quench the body's flame, lest this soul turns to ash.
Plunge me into the rapids of honeyed oblivion,
Sweet god of forgetfulness,
Lord of the lover's wet fire,
God of my infinite desire.
River Lethe, Lover Lethe,
I have cried
I have died

To drink of you.

Tonight your memory washes my soul

A warm rain tasting,

Wasting

No part of my hunger.

I dissolve into the silent thunder of your waters,

Wishing,

Drifting

On the wet wave of your thirst

Until I am river as you are river,

Submerged as you are submerged,

Holy as you are holy

In this star-fired night.

My life

Opens to your whisper;

Petal by petal,

Dream by dream,

You bloom the summer in me.

Breathless, with beating heart, I look down

From love's snow-shawled summit;

I have never been this close

To life,

To death,

To love...

I forget all fires, all voices

Calling from the grave of futility

And let this bounty, this beauty,

This heat, this terror,

This summer

Rage in me.

Formless as breath,

Dreamless as death,

Cold and mute as stone,

I am but pain's remembrance

Without your forgetfulness.

River Lethe, Lover Lethe,

I have cried,

I have died

To drink of you,

Only to be reborn,

Baptized by your shimmering soul

That upholds my reflection like a lantern.

River Lethe, Lover Lethe,

Far from the blind earth above,

I answer your call;

You are Love…you are Love, after all.

And I have cried

I have died

To drink of you.

Lover and man I now hold within me,

Adam scarred,

My Adam found…

Eden unbarred,

And unbound!

Fragrant earth, unbridled sea,

And wind-washed heavens know

Inside this barren life,

This body weary and worn,

A woman,

A woman has been born.

Declaration

I am a woman

Who has birthed my own suns

Danced my own dreams

Conquered my own abyss

I am a woman who has tasted life

The salt of blood and loss

And the bitter honey of unanswered prayer

I am a woman who owns her soul…lock and key

Her body…breast and bone

Her mind…thought and vision

I am a woman who has tamed the shadow

Invented a new self…times uncounted

Woven a tapestry of memory

I am a woman only beginning

Having ended so many times

I am a woman who has been here

And there is a scar

Where my fire has been

Earth Psalm

O Great Sculptor of Seasons,

We bow to Thy altars of green.

O Haunting Composer,

We sing with Thy choirs of wind, wave, and field.

O Eternal Creator,

We thank Thee for Thy artist's soul.

WinterSpeak

Encased in ice, I have learned to speak winter.

Sentenced to snow,

I have surrendered to cold chastity.

But in the heart of this tundra,

Behind stone that cannot burn,

A fire rages in your colors.

Resigned to paralysis,

I have married stillness.

But in the isolation of nights,

Behind stone that cannot move,

I dance barefoot to your summer.

Buried in white sleep,

I accept the sterile harvest.

But in the wasteland of want,

Behind stone that cannot hunger,

I ravage your orchards.

Enshrouded in futility,

I inherit compromise.

But in this prison of silence,

Behind stone that cannot speak,

I sing this love.

Wood Smoke

Prairie Fire

Sleep abandoned
My life like a prairie on fire with you
Drought upon drought
Waiting for rain
Blazing from a spark
Thrown by your eyes
Dark skies
Flaming like dawn
Love untouchable
Sleep abandoned
Thoughts like a prairie on fire with you
Love untouchable as an ember
And hard as a stone
Sleep abandoned
Glowing
Knowing
I do not burn alone

Indian Summer

I will remember this day

Of windswept gold

And the monarch with blowing wings

Pausing to drink from a flower-

The lake, a sapphire brushstroke

And the family, a trinity of smiles on its banks.

They, too, will remember this day,

The laughter and the tiny fish thrown back.

I hold this hour of final fruition

Scented with coming sleep.

Day of beautiful dying,

Burdened with the anguish of the grape

Being crushed between the hours,

And in the blue perfume of her grief,

The promise of wine.

Ruins

You entered my temple with soiled shoes

Destroyed sanctuary, shattered the mirror

Vomited the offerings and killed the Gods

Get out

I will not be a beggar in my own palace

Autobiography in Driftwood

Driftwood, refugee of the storm

Lost child of the forest, soft heart

Made wise and beautiful

In the harsh womb of the waters

A survivor of remembrance, this wood

Burnished and all too human

A life like mine

Which lends its voice

To the Inaudible.

What we are, the wave has made.

Home

Our kitchen smells like my mother's-
Olive oil and garlic, rosemary and browned butter,
And the scent of basil,
Bright and impossible to forget
Like the sweet earth of her smile.
Muffins rise in the oven;
Dinner simmers in reds of bell peppers and tomato.
You come in from outside,
And your hair is pungent
With early spring and wood smoke.
I inhale all of you as your arms draw me home.
How long I have traveled
To this house by the river
And this kitchen
That smells like my mother's…

Unfinished Web

Hour of silhouette

As the spider spins in the dusk

The place where lost things go

And dreams abandoned at the loom

Unlike the spider who weaves to completion

We begin selves that never bloom

Oh, to be like the spinner so sure of her silk

So sure of her house of Self

With no thought of other webs

Lost to the storm

No thought of dusk

The place where lost things go

And dreams abandoned at the loom

Spindrift

Somewhere purple flowers bloom
In the sand with strong shoulders
To battle the whims of the wind.
Somewhere twilight leaves her deepest
Shade of blue and drapes a veil
Of mist over the ocean's cerulean eyes.
Someday I will be buried there
With my unbreakable, rebellious lover,
The sea…
Where time has overlooked and stars
Reach down with silver hands
To touch where the surf has ebbed…
Where I can die only to return
With strong shoulders,
A sister of the dune flowers.

Elysium

Upon an unknown path, during a night's wandering,

I happened upon the Elysian Fields.

Unaware of my presence,

The Gods drank sunlight and supped on dreams

Lost by mortal men.

Sappho sang by a perfumed pool,

And nearby, Orpheus made his lyre weep.

In an orchard heavy with nectar, Leonardo

Painted an angel with azure eyes,

And with hair blown wild, Ludwig accompanied

The blue thunder of a waterfall.

In the distance, cloaked in solitude,

Poe drifted into gold mists with his gray eyes

Drunk with inspiration.

Emily plucked lilies from a rainbow garden

And pinned them to her white-clad bosom

As Shelley and Bryon drank wine from wild honeysuckle

And danced with the Muses.

Whitman dreamed with a youth

In dew-glimmering grass,

And Woolf waded in the waves

As Isadora danced in the foam,

Intoxicated by the opium of the siren's song.

Long hidden, long I watched them,

Gods now ignorant of time

And earthly fame burning steadily

In the world behind them.

Upon leaving, I wondered who will be next

To dance among them;

Who could dance among them?

Metaphysics

Cloud becomes rain

Rain becomes river

River becomes ocean

Ocean becomes cloud

Seed becomes tree

Tree becomes fruit

Fruit returns to soil

Soil cradles seed

The end becomes the beginning

Marlaina Donato

Poetry is the golden child of observation and catharsis-or so it is for poet-author-artist Marlaina Donato.

Her passion for words was sparked at age ten when her mother gave her a copy of Whitman's *Leaves of Grass*. Marlaina soon found her own Muse, scribbling onto bits of paper and in journals. Reading and writing poetry became necessity- bread for the soul and a compass to live by.

Marlaina lives in rural New Jersey with her husband Joe and their canine muse Noah.

Contact: Ekstasis Multimedia, LLC at www.booksandbrush.net

www.ingramcontent.com/pod-product-compliance
Lightning Source LLC
Chambersburg PA
CBHW071415040426
42444CB00009B/2261